Reading
BOROUGH COUNCIL

KT-419-120

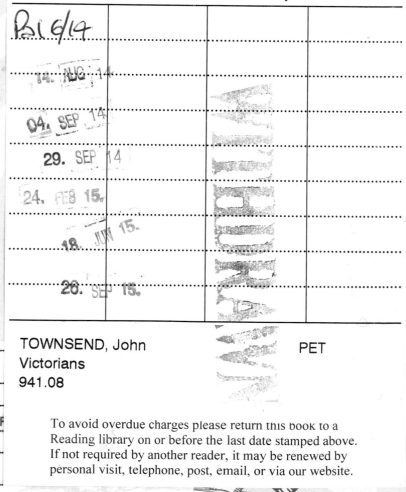

LONDON•SYDNEY

First published in 2013 by Franklin Watts

Created and developed by Taglines Creative Limited
Text by John Townsend
Illustrations and layout by Matt Lilly
Cover design by Cathryn Gilbert

Franklin Watts
338 Euston Road London NW1 3BH

Franklin Watts Australia
Level 17/207 Kent Street, Sydney, NSW 2000

A CIP catalogue record for this book
is available from the British Library.

(ebook) ISBN: 978 1 4451 2239 7
(PB) ISBN 978 1 4451 2193 2
(Library ebook) ISBN 978 1 4451 2582 4

1 3 5 7 9 10 8 6 4 2

Picture credits:
p.8 Georgios Kollidas/Shutterstock; p.11 Georgios Kollidas /Shutterstock;
p.12 Donna Beeler/Shutterstock; p.19 Morphart Creation/Shutterstock; p.20
f9photos/Shutterstock p.26 chippix/Shutterstock;
p.38 Bram van Broekhoven/Shutterstock; p.40 Nicku/Shutterstock;
p.41 Stephen Finn/Shutterstock; p.74 Dr Jools/Shutterstock;
p.82 petejeff/Shutterstock; p.87 LiliGraphie/Shutterstock;
p.53 The Print Collector/Alamy; p84 GL Archive/Alamy;
pp.42–43 Dave Clancy/nswrecks.netp.67; Tyne & Wear Archive & Museum

Every attempt has been made to clear copyright on the photographs
reproduced in this book. Any omissions, please apply to the
Publisher for rectification.

Printed and bound by CPI Group (UK) Ltd, Croydon, CR0 4YY

Franklin Watts is
a division of Hachette Children's Books,
an Hachette UK company.

www.hachette.co.uk

CONTENTS

Chapter 1: Vintage Victorians   6

Who was Victoria?   8

Victoria – the Soap, Episode 1: The Queen
        and the Prince   10

How bad could it be?   12

Chapter 2: Mad Moments   14

Maddening manners   16

Keep covered!   18

Crushing corsets   20

Victoria – the Soap, Episode 2: Mad
        Murder Attempts   22

Survival Quiz 1   24

Chapter 3: Bad Times for Children   26

Woeful work   28

Mad and miserable   30

Scary schools   32

Victoria – the Soap, Episode 3: Royal Children   34

Survival Quiz 2   36

Chapter 4: Dangerous Travels   38

Train terrors   40

Perishing sea steamers   42

Disastrous day out   44

Survival Quiz 3   46

Chapter 5: Mad Medicine   **48**

Daring doctors   50

Nutty nurses   52

Victoria – the Soap, Episode 4: Disease

      and Death   54

Grisly germs   55

Survival Quiz 4   58

Chapter 6: Bad Behaviour   **60**

Bonkers bobbies   62

Mad murderers   64

Unlucky urchins   66

Incredible hulks   68

Survival Quiz 5   70

Chapter 7: Dangerous Dragons' Den!   **72**

Ingenious inventions   74

Survival Quiz 6   80

Chapter 8: Final Fate   **82**

Victoria – the Soap, Episode 5: Final Farewell   84

Fatal finish   86

Survival Quiz Results   88

Dramatic Dates   90

Gruesome Glossary   92

Weird Websites   93

Infernal Index   94

Read on before it's too late!

Chapter 1
Vintage Victorians

Over 150 years ago, Queen Victoria ruled when Britain was becoming rich and powerful. Dirty, crowded cities grew around the new factories that began the Industrial Revolution. This brought great wealth to the few people who owned the businesses, but for most poor Victorians, life could be mad, bad and just plain dangerous.

We Victorians love babies. This is my twelfth.

Welcome, to all you historians

To the world of the
vintage Victorians

Who were mad, bad
and scary,

Big-whiskered and hairy
(and that's just the ladies)

Or stuffy and stern-faced
STRICT-orians!

Who was Victoria?

Victoria was born in 1819, the only child of the Duke and Duchess of Kent. Her uncle, King William IV, died just after Victoria's 18th birthday, so she was old enough to take over the throne. Many people thought she would make a terrible leader because she was so young and a female! To find out more, watch out for *Victoria – the Soap*, beginning on page 10.

Cast list:

Victoria   1837–1901

Prince Albert (her husband)   1819–1861

John Brown   1826–1883
**(personal servant and close
friend of the Queen)**

Victoria's mum   1786–1861
(Duchess of Kent)

**The Lord Chamberlain, several doctors
and lots of babies.**

Victoria, here! I'm only 1.4 metres tall so I might need to stand on a box.

Victoria — quick facts

 Victoria didn't like to get too warm. She kept the windows open (even in winter) and had ice on the dinner table to keep the room cool.

 Victoria survived at least seven assassination attempts. Three of her attackers were found to be insane and sent to mental asylums.

 Eight of Victoria's children 'sat on the thrones of Europe'. That's a lot of sitting around!

 Victoria kept diaries throughout her life, which fill about 120 volumes.

Prince William and Prince Harry are the great-great-great-great grandsons of Queen Victoria.

> I'd be a great blogger but it hasn't been invented yet.

Victoria  the Soap

Episode 1: The Queen and the Prince

Scene 1: Kensington Palace, London. Victoria is in bed. Her mother rushes in. Date: June 20th 1837, time 6.30am.

Action

Mother: Victoria, wake up. The Lord Chamberlain is here to see you.

Chamberlain: We have news, Princess Alexandrina Victoria…

Victoria: Just call me Vicky.

Chamberlain: Not any more, Your Highness. The king, your uncle, died this morning so you are now *Queen*.

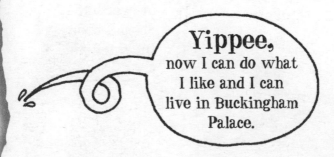

Yippee, now I can do what I like and I can live in Buckingham Palace.

Scene 2: Two years later at Balmoral Castle, Scotland.

Action

Victoria:	Hello, Cousin Albert. I'm now the Queen of Great Britain and Ireland and the whole British Empire.
Albert:	Das ist gut. (That is good.)
Victoria:	Sie sind nett. (You are nice.)
Albert:	Ich liebe Sie. (I love you.)
Victoria:	Heirate mich. (Marry me.)
Albert:	Yay! (I'm in luck.)

When Queen Victoria married Albert in 1840, she wore a white satin dress. She started a trend because before this wedding gowns were made in all colours.

I cut quite the dashing figure, ja!

How bad could it be?

Unlike the super-rich royals, many Victorians lived in slums. In the poorest areas, sometimes as many as 1 in every 3 babies died before they were a year old. Diseases spread quickly in overcrowded towns so death was all around.

We're a happy family really. Shame one of us is dead.

I think it might be me.

Some families spent their savings on a photo of a dead loved one. The dead were propped up and often had their eyes pinned open to make them look as if they were still alive. Mad or what!

Soggy body

Few poor people could afford coffins, so bodies
often ended up in a river. Men called 'dredgermen'
collected soggy bodies from the river and handed
them to the police. They were paid for each
corpse they collected.

I've fished out two feet, a hand, a head and two arms.

That's nearly some body. Half pay!

Chapter 2

MAD Moments

The Victorians were very concerned about 'class'. The upper classes thought it was not proper to show emotion in public. They had to keep a 'stiff upper lip' and never make a fuss. There were lots of other mad rules for almost everything...

Victorian manners
and snobbery

Were madness — like murder
and robbery!

So much was forbidden

Or hushed-up and hidden

And kisses could never
be slobbery!

Maddening manners

In 'respectable' homes, rules for children were very strict.

One for Mama, one for Papa, one for Grandmama, one for...

 Never argue with your elders — they always know best.

 Children should be seen and not heard.

Never allow your parents to bring you a chair and never allow them to get one for themselves.

 Never run up and down stairs or across the room.

Always do as you are told in a pleasant and willing way.

 Always stand when visitors arrive.

Take a seat

A gentleman always had to take off his hat when he entered a room, even if the room was empty. If a lady entered the room, he had to offer her his chair. If his seat was still warm, he had to get her another chair as it was disgusting to ask a lady to sit on a chair still warm from a man's bottom!

How dare you burp before my wife!

I do apologise. I didn't know it was her turn.

Keep covered!

Respectable Victorian ladies could never show any part of their legs in public — even at the seaside. Rich people paid to get changed inside bathing machines, which were wooden huts on wheels. The huts were pulled down the beach into the sea by a horse.

Men and women often had to bathe in different parts of the beach, sometimes separated by a fence.

Oooh, ankles!

When crossing the street, Victorian ladies were not supposed to lift their dress with both hands as too much ankle would show. The myth grew that Victorians were so shocked by seeing ankles and legs that they even covered up the legs of tables! In fact, it was just the fashion to cover furniture with fancy cloths, lace and embroidery.

I'm just going to have a bath.

Make sure you cover your ankles.

Crushing corsets

Hourglass figures were the hot new fashion for women in the 1850s. Corsets made with whale bones, steel and string gave women a slim waist. Some reports tell of corsets squeezing waists to a tiny 40 centimetres or less. Yikes! Strapping on a bustle under a dress also helped to create the ideal figure by making ladies' bottoms look bigger.

MAD

I do hope my bum looks big in this!

hourglass

Not just for girls...

Girls as young as three could be laced up into corsets made from whale bones. These corsets made breathing difficult and might even damage a girl's internal organs — so Victorian women were well-known for fainting or 'getting the vapours'. Oh, yes ... and men sometimes wore corsets, too ...

CORSETS for men

Because you're worth it!

Before

After

Victoria  the Soap

Episode 2: Mad Murder Attempts

Scene 1: Victoria and Albert are in an open carriage driving through London. Date: 1840.

Action

Victoria: I'm so happy. I'm expecting our first child. I say, look at that young man stepping out.

Albert: Oh no, he has a gun. Get down! (*BANG, BANG*)

Victoria: Gosh! That was lucky – he missed.

The young man was 18-year-old Edward Oxford who was arrested at the scene. He was locked up in Bedlam Asylum for being mentally ill.

> Look at the dust down here, Albert – I am not amused!

Scene 2: Two years later in The Mall, London.

Victoria: Eek, there's another man with a gun!

(*BANG, BANG*). He's escaped!

The police had a plan to catch the killer. They asked Victoria to make the same journey the next day. It worked! John Francis tried to shoot Victoria again and the police caught him. As well as these mad assassination attempts, a crazy man once chased Victoria's carriage claiming that she stole the throne from him!

Team up with friends or try the quiz yourself to see if you would survive in Victorian times. Add up your scores for each answer. When you've done all the quizzes, check out the final results on page 88.

1. Do you ever run up or down stairs?

A Never

B Only if I'm in a hurry

C All the time

2. Do you let adults hear you speaking?

A Yes

B No

C Who cares?

3. Do you stand up when a visitor enters the room?

A Whatever for?

B Always

C No

Scores for answers:

1. A = 9 B = 5 C = 0 (You could be punished for doing this)

2. A = 0 B = 10 C = 2 (You could be punished for doing this)

3. A = 5 B = 10 C = 0 (You could be punished for not doing this)

Chapter 3

BAD Times for Children

Growing up in Victorian times was grim for poor children. They would often have to do hard, dangerous work for little pay. For those who went to school, cruel teachers, horrible lessons and painful punishments could make learning a misery. Even the royal children had bad times as their mother could be scarily strict.

> Oh, no! I've got years of mad, bad and dangerous Victorian childhood ahead of me!

Victorian children, beware...

There are dangerous places
out there,

Where nasty things lurk

At home, school and work

And a beating awaits
everywhere!

Woeful work

Poor children were often sent out to earn money doing dangerous or even deadly jobs.

In 1833, the first Factory Act was passed to stop children under the age of 9 from working. Other Acts followed:

 1842 Mines Act — no child under the age of 10 to work underground in a coal mine.

 1847 Ten Hour Act — no child to work more than 10 hours in a day.

 1874 Factory Act — no child under the age of 9 to be employed in a factory.

I knew I should have lied about my age!

Fire below!

A chimney-sweep boy wasn't fed much, keeping him skinny enough to squeeze up narrow chimneys. If he got stuck, his master would poke a long stick up the chimney to prod him, or even light a fire underneath to get him moving!

I'm at the top of my career.

Children and adults who worked in hat factories often got mercury poisoning, which could harm their brains. 'As mad as a hatter' became a saying, and inspired the character of the Mad Hatter in the Victorian book *Alice's Adventures in Wonderland*.

Mad and miserable

Victorian London's East End was very poor, with many children living on the streets. Some orphans lived in workhouses, but others had to beg or become 'crossing sweepers'. These children swept away the horse poo and dirt from the paths of rich people crossing the street.

I'm going to need a bigger brush!

In 1867, Thomas Barnardo set up the Ragged School to help the neglected children of East London. Today, Barnardo's is a charity that still helps children and young people.

Match catch

Many of the children who worked in London's match factories developed 'phossy jaw' from working with white phosphorus. Their teeth, gums and jaws became badly deformed with painful abcesses full of foul-smelling pus. Brain damage and other illness led to death. By the 1890s, new match factories stopped using deadly white phosphorus. Matches were sold on the streets by young match sellers.

Scary schools

Many poor families sent their children to work instead of school even though, by law, children aged between 5 and 10 had to attend school. The leaving age was raised to 11 in 1893. But going to school was almost as scary as work.

Left-handed children could be punished for not using their right hand. Children who were slow to learn might have to wear a dunce's hat and stand in a corner for everyone to see.

Why have I got a D on my hat when my name's Tom?

Hold out your hand...

Teachers had even more painful ways to punish children. A cane was kept in every classroom — always at the ready. The cane was used to strike a child's hand or bottom, or the back of their legs. Sometimes, a leather strap was used instead of the cane. In public schools, prefects could cane younger pupils. Yikes!

Victoria the Soap

Episode 3: Royal Children

Scene: Buckingham Palace with Queen Victoria.

Date: 1857.

Victoria:	My ninth child! I don't even like children. They wear me out. After all, it's me who keeps them in order.
Albert:	You can be a little strict, my love.
Victoria:	Get out, Albert! Go to your room.

Later, a note comes under Victoria's door.

Victoria:	Hmm, another note from Albert. He says mother is coming to see me.
Victoria's mother:	*(Sweeping in)* All your children are crying. You really shouldn't beat little Leopold quite so much. He's a sick child.
Victoria:	I don't want him turning out like his spoilt older brother, Bertie.

Mother:	And I think you scare Albert when you shout at the children.
Victoria:	Too bad! Hmm, maybe I should draw up a list of the children to help me remember them all.

Victoria's checklist

BORN	NAME
1840	Victoria (Princess Royal – Vicky)
1841	Edward (Bertie) – Prince of Wales
1843	Alice
1844	Alfred
1846	Helena
1848	Louise
1850	Arthur
1853	Leopold (invalid/haemophiliac)
1857	Beatrice

SURVIVAL QUIZ 2

Team up with friends or try the quiz yourself to see if you would survive in Victorian times. Add up your scores for each answer. When you've done all the quizzes, check out the final results on page 88.

%%%%%%%%%%%%%%

1. Are you scared of the dark?

A Yes — eek!

B Sometimes

C I like the dark

2. Are you left-handed?

A Yes

B No

C Not sure

3. Do you annoy teachers?

A Never

B Often

C All the time

Scores for answers:

1. A = 0 B = 5 C = 9 (You might have to work down a mine or up a chimney)

2. A = 2 B = 9 C = 5 (Left-handed children could be beaten by teachers)

3. A = 8 B = 3 C = 0 (You'd be at risk of getting the cane or a good thrashing)

%%%%%%%%%%%%%

Chapter 4
DANGEROUS Travels

There were so many horses in Victorian London that it became very difficult to get around. There were carriages everywhere and piles of smelly horse dung. Steam engines came to the rescue — steam trains and boats let more people travel further than ever before. But rail travel was far more mad and dangerous than today...

Hold tight — we're coming off the rails!

With railways and ships at
full steam,

Victorians travelled their
dream...

Touring further and faster

They risked sure disaster...

Hold tight – as the next bit
could well make you scream!

Train terrors

In 1865, the famous Victorian author Charles Dickens survived a bad train crash.

He was on a train that came off the tracks after running into engineering works at Staplehurst in Kent. Ten people died and 49 were injured. Dickens helped some of the injured before climbing back into the wrecked carriage to rescue the manuscript of his latest novel (*Our Mutual Friend*). His writing was soon back on track.

> What the Dickens is all the fuss about?

Off the rails

In 1878, in a violent storm, the Tay Railway Bridge collapsed just as a train to Dundee was going over it. The whole train plunged into the river killing everyone on board. About 75 people were on the train, but only 46 bodies were ever found. The cause of the crash wasn't just the wind. The bridge had been poorly built and maintained.

This new Tay Bridge is so solid it will last forever.

Er... I felt it move ... quick, run...

Perishing sea steamers

Each year thousands of Victorians left Britain to find their fortunes in America. The SS *Atlantic* was one of the steam ships that made regular trips between Liverpool and New York.

In the early morning of 1st April 1873, just off the coast of North America, the ship struck an underwater ledge and sank. All the lifeboats were washed away. One of the crew managed to swim to a rock where he tied a line to help passengers get to shore.

Saved from the waves

Of the 952 people on board, 562 drowned in the
icy cold water. No women or children survived
— apart from John Hindley, a 12-year-old boy.
He clung to a mast poking above the waves and
was eventually rescued by a local clergyman in a
rowing boat. John's story became so well known in
America that the famous Barnum Circus wanted to
put him in a show as 'The Orphan of the Wreck!'

Disastrous day out

The *Princess Alice* was a paddle steamer on the River Thames. In 1878, she left London Bridge at 10am on a day trip to Gravesend, packed with families and children.

The Bywell Castle

Between 750 and 800 passengers were on board. The journey out went to plan, but as the boat headed back in the evening, disaster struck.

The Bywell Castle, a coal ship, crashed into the *Princess Alice* and cut her almost in half. She sank in four minutes. Passengers were trapped below decks or thrown into the river. The water was so polluted and stinking that no one stood much chance of surviving. Only 69 people were saved. Hundreds of bodies were recovered, but some were never found.

Princess Alice

SURVIVAL QUIZ 3

Team up with friends or try the quiz yourself to see if you would survive in Victorian times. Add up your scores for each answer. When you've done all the quizzes, check out the final results on page 88.

1. Would you want to go on a steam train?

A You bet!

B I'd give it a try

C No, thanks

2. Would you want to go on a steam ship?

A Not likely

B You bet!

C I'd give it a try

3. Would you try to swim away from a sinking ship on the River Thames?

A Never

B Of course

C I can't swim

Scores for answers:

1. A = 3 B = 5 C = 9 (Victorian rail travel could be risky)

2. A = 9 B = 3 C = 5 (Victorian steam ships could be risky)

3. A = 6 B = 1 C = 4 (Swimming in filthy Victorian rivers was usually fatal)

47

Chapter 5

MAD Medicine

Medical treatments could be very scary in early Victorian times. Doctors didn't know about germs and they didn't realise many diseases were spread in dirty water and sewers. Surgeons didn't know about keeping wounds clean, and patients often died from infection. But some doctors were coming up with 'mad' ideas that would make medicine much safer for the future.

When Victorians felt
really queasy

Or sneezy, uneasy
and wheezy

It may have been due

To the slum outside loo...

Very sleazy, diseasey
and breezy!

Daring doctors

Removing a diseased limb was terrifying in Victorian times. The surgeon had to cut quickly with a knife and a saw while the patient was held down, screaming. The surgeon, Robert Liston (1794–1847), was proud of how quickly he could remove a patient's leg.

A story tells how Liston was so fast in one operation that he cut off the patient's leg and his assistant's fingers. The patient and the assistant later died from infections in the hospital.

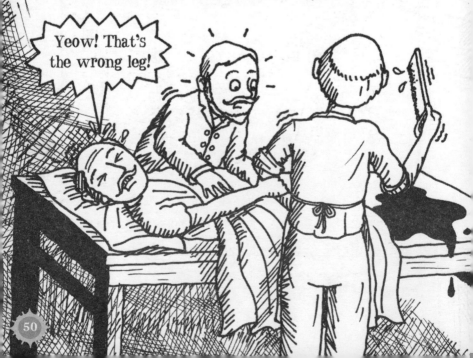

Yeow! That's the wrong leg!

You won't feel a thing...

James Young Simpson (1811—1870) was a Scottish surgeon who was interested in anaesthetics. One night in 1847, he asked friends round to experiment with the gas called 'chloroform'. They all passed out and fell under the table.

A year earlier, Robert Liston used an anaesthetic called 'ether' in a public operation in London. Pain-free operations had begun.

Nutty nurses

In 1854, British soldiers fought against Russia in the Crimean War in Turkey. So many soldiers were badly injured that women were asked to help look after them. When nurse Florence Nightingale went there to manage a ward for wounded soldiers, the doctors were in for a surprise.

But women can't run a hospital ... they're just women...

And they're bound to faint at the sight of all this blood ... oh, I feel sick...

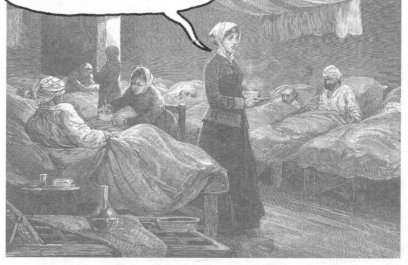

The first requirement of a hospital is that it should do the sick no harm.

Hospital horrors

The hospital in Turkey was filthy. More soldiers were dying from diseases such as typhoid, cholera and dysentery than from their war wounds. Florence and her nurses set up a kitchen, dug proper toilets and kept everything clean.

Fewer soldiers died and Florence's work was no longer seen as mad, but amazing. Florence decided all nurses should be properly trained. In 1860, she set up the Nightingale Training School for nurses in London.

Victoria  the Soap

Episode 4: Disease and Death

Scene 1: Windsor Castle. Prince Albert lies in bed. His breathing is slow, his skin pale and sweaty. The queen holds his hand and sobs. Date: 14th December, 1861.

Action

Doctor: *(Whispering)* We fear the prince has typhoid fever, Your Majesty.

Victoria: Can't you do something to make him better?

Doctor: I'll give him more brandy.

Albert: Too late. I'm going…. ergh grmph zzzz *(dies)*

Victoria: NO! Aaaaaagh!

Prince Albert was buried nine days later.
Queen Victoria was too grief-stricken to
attend the funeral.

What now for Queenie?
Find out on page 84…

Grisly germs

Typhoid was a common killer in Victorian times. It was caught from food or drink handled by someone who carried the disease, or from sewage getting into drinking water. Yuk! Most doctors thought it was caused by breathing in smelly air.

Killer cholera

In 1854, an outbreak of cholera killed over 600 people in London. Dr John Snow (1813–1858) believed the disease was spread in water. He discovered a mother had washed a dirty nappy at a street water pump and contaminated it. He had the pump closed and cholera cases stopped.

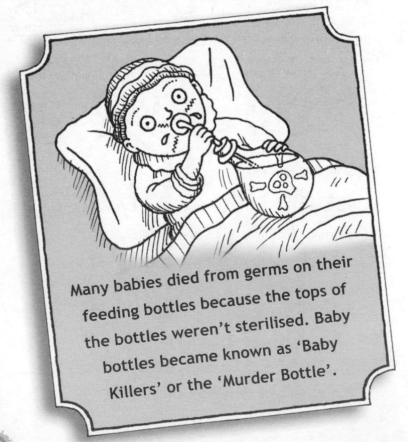

Many babies died from germs on their feeding bottles because the tops of the bottles weren't sterilised. Baby bottles became known as 'Baby Killers' or the 'Murder Bottle'.

Stinky sewage

In Victorian times all raw sewage from homes, factories and slaughter houses ended up in the River Thames. In the hot summer of 1858, the sewage was at its worst. The people of London could hardly breathe from the stench of the filthy water. It became known as 'The Great Stink'. Deadly germs were flowing through London under everyone's noses. PHEWEE!

Team up with friends or try the quiz yourself to see if you would survive in Victorian times. Add up your scores for each answer. When you've done all the quizzes, check out the final results on page 88.

1. Have you ever been to hospital?

A No

B Just once

C Lots

2. Have you ever drunk water from a tap or pump?

A Of course

B No, only bottles

C Who cares?

3. Do you always wash your hands and use antibacterial soap?

A No

B Always

C Now and again

Scores for answers:

1. A = 10 B = 4 C = 0 (If you had to go to a Victorian hospital you might not come out)
2. A = 1 B = 9 C = 2 (If you drank from Victorian pipes, it could be risky)
3. A = 2 B = 9 C = 5 (Many Victorians didn't know dirty hands spread germs)

Chapter 6

BAD Behaviour

Crime was a huge problem for the Victorians. As cities got bigger, with even more people on the streets, thieves had greater opportunities. Some homeless children could only survive by stealing food. But as the police force grew, so did the chances of getting caught ... with scary prisons and punishments waiting.

You ain't catchin' me!

Victorian crime was a worry

When rapscallions struck
   in a flurry!

Such skulking skulduggery

And scallywag thuggery

Crammed prisons chock-full
   in a hurry.

Bonkers Bobbies

Victorian policemen were called 'Peelers' or
'Bobbies' after Sir Robert Peel, who formed
the London police force in 1829. Early Victorian
police worked seven days a week for just £1.
They couldn't vote and needed permission to get
married! Each officer had a wooden truncheon
carried in a long pocket in the tail of his coat.
They also carried a pair of handcuffs and
a wooden rattle to raise the alarm. By the 1880s,
the rattle had been replaced by a whistle.

Death by hanging

During most of Victoria's long reign there were 222 crimes that were punishable by hanging, including:

- Being in the company of gypsies for a month.
- Damaging Westminster Bridge.
- 'Strong evidence of malice' in children aged 7–14.
- Stealing from a shipwreck.
- Writing a threatening letter.
- Stealing from a rabbit warren.
- Begging without a licence if you were a soldier or sailor.
- Poaching.

Hang him!

But I didn't know poaching eggs was a crime...

Mad murderers

Mary Ann Cotton was Britain's worst serial killer of the 19th century. When her third husband died suddenly the police began asking questions. Mary Ann was found guilty of poisoning up to 21 people, including ten of her children, three husbands, five stepchildren and her mother. She was hanged in 1873 aged 40.

Have some more cornflakes, dear.

No thanks, you're a cereal killer.

Arsenic was sold in shops and used as cheap face powder or rat poison. But it was handy for murderers because it had no taste or smell when mixed with food or drink.

Jack's back!

Between August and November of 1888 terror struck the foggy cobbled streets of Whitechapel in London. At least five women were horribly murdered by the same vicious killer, nicknamed Jack the Ripper. All the victims had their throats cut and some of their organs removed. The killer was never caught and police never knew why he killed his victims. There were many suspects but no one really knows who he was.

I kill my victims with a smoked herring. Yes, I'm Jack the Kipper.

Unlucky urchins

Many young orphans became street urchins who stole food to survive or joined pickpocket gangs run by adult thieves. 'Mudlarks' were poor children who waded in the mud beside the River Thames in London, looking for lost rings or bits of scrap metal to sell so they could buy food.

My name is Ellen and I am 11. I was accused of stealing iron and given a week's hard labour.

Grim times

If children misbehaved in prison they were put on a diet of bread and water. They were sometimes put in solitary confinement. That meant being locked in a cell alone without any light for a long time. If they still caused trouble, young prisoners, especially boys, would be tied in a straitjacket and strapped to the wall in a standing position for up to six hours.

Incredible hulks

Victorian prisons became badly overcrowded. What could be done with so many prisoners? Answer: put them on ships. Prison ships or 'hulks' were anchored along river banks and at ports. Conditions on board were worse than the grimmest prisons on land. With prisoners packed together, many were killed by deadly diseases, such as typhoid and cholera. During the day, prisoners had to do back-breaking work on the docks or dredge the rivers. At night they were chained to their bunks.

Help –
I'm drowning!
I started to dig an
escape tunnel...

Wish I wasn't here...

Many convicts were sent to Australia. The boat journey took about six months and prisoners were locked in iron cages in filthy conditions.

Are we nearly there yet?

From 1787 to 1857, 162,000 British convicts were transported to Australia. Some were as young as nine or ten, and a few were over 80! This stopped by 1857 because Australians were fed up with so many British convicts arriving.

SURVIVAL QUIZ 5

Team up with friends or try the quiz yourself to see if you would survive in Victorian times. Add up your scores for each answer. When you've done all the quizzes, check out the final results on page 88.

1. If you were starving, would you ever steal food?

A No problem

B Never

C Only if I was desperate

2. Would you ever take anything from a wrecked ship?

A Yes

B No

C Only if it was something I wanted

3. Would you like a one-way ticket to Australia?

A Never

B You bet

C I'd only want a return ticket

Scores for answers:

1. A = 1 B = 10 C = 4 (Victorian thieves could be seriously punished or executed)

2. A = 0 B = 10 C = 2 (Victorian children could be hanged for this!)

3. A = 2 B = 8 C = 0 (Victorians could be sent to Australia and never see home again)

Chapter 7

DANGEROUS

Dragons' Den!

The Victorians came up with all sorts of new ideas, from the wild and wacky to the dodgy and daft. Victorians invented lots of great things, from cameras, bicycles and typewriters to electric lights, telephones and radio transmitters. But not everyone at the time thought these were good ideas...

A telephone? It'll never catch on!

Ladies loved a Victorian invention

With its cistern and chain in suspension,

But often they blushed

And felt rather flushed...

What was it? It's best not to mention!

(But read on to find out...)

Ingenious inventions

Invention 1: Stamp licker

The newly invented Penny Black stamp is essential for sending out Christmas cards (another Victorian invention). It has a picture of Her Majesty on the front, but it needs a sticky backside (the stamp, not Her Majesty). A new idea is to have gummed stamps that become sticky when you lick them. If you have lots of cards to send, you may want to invest in A STAMP LICKER!

water

brush

I get my butler to lick 'em.

It'll never catch on.

Who's Penny Black?

Philately gets you nowhere!

Invention 2: Flushing water closet

I'm Thomas Twyford and I've built the first one-piece, all china toilet. The internal workings of this cutting-edge water closet flushes away waste into our new Victorian sewers (and into the river!) Great, eh?

Will you invest, or has the bottom fallen out of the market?

Loo-dicrous. It's money down the drain.

Bog standard idea.

Not much to go on.

It stinks!

Invention 3: Sea boots

Have you ever dreamed of walking on water?
How about these sensational sea boots? You can
save a fortune on boat fares... just stroll over
the river, or even across The Channel to France!

Invention 4:
All-weather unicycle

Raindrops (don't) keep falling on my head!

spokes

Who cares about rain with this unicycle designed with an on-board umbrella! Unlike the more wobbly penny-farthing bicycle, this machine protects the rider with spokes. It's also useful for transporting prisoners as it's almost impossible to get out of!

Bonkers.

I'll make you an offer ... here's some arsenic.

Mad, or what?

Brilliant! I love it.

Invention 5:
Moustache protector

Just what every Victorian needs — but maybe not
one for the ladies! This clever invention will stop
your moustache getting in the soup and becoming
jammed up with, er, jam. No more need for
napkins... just nip under the tablecloth and apply
it before eating.

Rubbish idea!

Needs a stiff upper lip.

Will it tickle your nose?

I like it!

Invention 6: Hands-free reader

Too cold to read at night? Hands getting tired of holding a book? Stock up on the latest Dickens novel, Sherlock Holmes mystery or Charles Darwin's *The Origin of Species*. You can now read them all in bed and keep your hands nice and warm under the bedclothes (except to turn the page).

Ha, ha! Hee, hee!

We'll take that as a 'NO', then!

Team up with friends or try the quiz yourself to see if you would survive in Victorian times. Add up your scores for each answer. When you've done all the quizzes, check out the final results on page 88.

1. Do you depend on your phone?

A All the time

B Never

C Now and again

2. Would you like to ride a penny-farthing bicycle?

A I might give it a try

B Not likely

C Definitely

3. Would you try to walk on water in sea boots?

A No, thanks

B You bet

C Only with a life jacket

Scores for answers:

1. A = 0 B = 9 C = 5 (Victorians didn't use phones — only just invented)

2. A = 2 B = 10 C = 0 (Victorians kept falling off and often got badly hurt)

3. A = 9 B = 1 C = 4 (Don't be fooled by the picture — these were mega risky)

Chapter 8
Final Fate

With their fascination for ghosts, murder stories
and tales of body-snatching, the Victorians
spent a lot of time thinking about death!
Many Victorian writers wrote spooky stories
and plays to scare everyone. After all, death was
everywhere and it was taken very seriously.
So for the last word from the Victorians, we go
to the final episode of Victoria's life and maybe
a message from beyond the grave...

Hello...
Is anybody
there?

Grave robbers in foggy
gaslight

Snatched bodies from
coffins at night...

Victorian tales

Told grisly details...

SO BEWARE... (but if you're
alive, you're all right!)

Victoria  the Soap

Episode 5: Final Farewell

Scene 1: Windsor Castle. John Brown looks unwell.

Date: 1883.

> What fine fetlocks and withers, your Majesty.

> Thank you, John. It's all down to my new corset.

Action

John Brown:	Your Highness, I have a wee chill.
Victoria:	It's just a draught under your kilt. You've been such a good friend to me since Albert died.
John Brown:	I really must get to my bed, ma'am.
	A few days later
Victoria:	Oh, no! John is dead. I am heart-broken.

Scene 2: Osborne House, Isle of Wight. Victoria has been in bed for days. Date: January, 1901.

Victoria:	*(Mumbling)* Albert, my Albert… I still miss you. And you John…
Doctor Reid:	Your Highness, are you feeling all right?
Victoria:	I am slipping away… ergh *(she dies)*
Doctor Reid (to the audience):	Her Majesty told me to place these in her coffin: Albert's dressing gown, a plaster cast of Albert's hand, and photographs…

I'll take my secret to the grave…

He places <u>Queen Victoria's</u> wedding veil over her face and puts a picture of John Brown in her right hand, which he covers with flowers.

The Victorian period was over… what came next is another story!

The end!

Fatal finish

One of the big fears for many Victorians was being buried alive. Some diseases, such as cholera, could make victims appear to be dead, when they weren't.

Victorian inventors came to the rescue with all sorts of gadgets, such as the 'safety coffin' fitted with bells, whistles, air-tubes and flags just in case the body woke up. If it did, the movement of the body triggered the opening of an air pipe that made a flag stand up above ground. Let's hope someone was looking!

Just checking

Another type of safety coffin was attached to a tube that gravediggers or priests could look through and check every few hours after the funeral. If they saw anything move or couldn't smell any rotting, they had to dig up the grave immediately. Apparently, one inventor showed off his safety coffin by burying himself alive in it, to be fed sausages and soup through the feeding tube. Nice!

How can I make sure I'm not buried alive?

Climb in with the lions at London Zoo.

What is your total score from the Survival Quizzes at the end of the chapters? Add up your points from all 18 questions to see how long you would survive in the Victorian age.

Over 150 WOW — you'd make a great Victorian! Your chances of making it to old age are promising. Then again, were all your answers strictly honest?

100 — 150 Fairly good. You're a Victorian with a fair chance of reaching middle age with a smile.

80 — 100 Not bad. You'd make a fairly average Victorian but don't plan for old age.

50 — 80 Oo-er — you're high risk. Victorian life isn't for you. You have seriously low 19th century survival chances.

Below 50 AAH! Give up now. You wouldn't make a successful Victorian. Only a miserably dead one.

If your scores were a whole mixture, that means you'd probably be a fairly normal Victorian. You'd have no idea if or when something horrible would strike... like being buried alive! In fact, Robert Liston or Jack the Ripper might already be sharpening their knives just for you...

Why is Queen Victoria like a measuring stick?

Because she was a very long ruler.

Dramatic Dates

1837   Queen Victoria is crowned, aged 18 years.
Many people think the job is too great for her
as she is so young, but she is determined to
prove them wrong.

1840   Queen Victoria marries her first cousin,
Prince Albert. The Penny Black stamp is
issued – the first postage stamp in the world.

1841   The royal couple's second child (and heir to the
throne) Albert Edward ('Bertie') is born.

1843   Charles Dickens publishes *A Christmas Carol*.
It sells out in six days.

1842   The Mines Act stops children under 10 from
working in the mines.

1845–52 Ireland suffers the Great Potato Famine when
whole crops of potatoes are ruined by a fungus.
About 800,000 people die from starvation. Many
move to Britain, the US, Canada and Australia.

1852   The first public flushing toilet opens in London.

1854   Florence Nightingale goes to the Crimea,
Turkey (now within Ukraine), to organise
nursing during the war.

1860s   The 'boneshaker' appears on the roads – one
of the first bicycles to have pedals to turn the
front wheels.

1861   Death of Prince Albert aged 42 years.

1868 Michael Barrett was the last man to be hanged in public in England for his part in the Clerkenwell bombing which killed 12 bystanders. Barrett had planted the bomb in a wheelbarrow outside a prison to help others escape.

1872 The first F.A. Cup Final is held.

1876 Alexander Graham Bell invents the telephone.

1877 Queen Victoria becomes Empress of India.

1880 Children up to the age of 10 now have to go to school.

1883 John Brown, the Queen's personal servant, dies aged 56.

1896 The speed limit for the first cars in Britain is raised from 4 mph to 14 mph (6 kph to 22.5 kph).

1897 Queen Victoria's Diamond Jubilee (Queen for 60 years).

1901 Queen Victoria dies after ruling longer than any other British monarch. Her eldest son 'Bertie' becomes ruler as King Edward Vll.

Gruesome Glossary

anaesthetic a chemical or gas that sends someone into deep sleep. It is used by surgeons before they perform operations

assassination attempts trying to kill an important person

bustle a pad or frame worn under a skirt (over the bottom), to make the dress puff out behind

chloroform a liquid with a strong vapour (gas) once used to put patients into a deep sleep before surgery

class (social class) the group that people belong to based on their work and wealth: e.g. lower class, middle class and upper class

cobbled streets roads made of small rounded bricks or stones

contaminated polluted

dysentery an illness caused by bacteria, giving major stomach upsets and blood in poo

ether a liquid once used by doctors before surgery to put patients into a deep sleep

haemophilia a disease in which the blood fails to clot – even a small cut can cause death. It usually only affects males and is passed on by women to their male children

hard labour punishment for criminals by making them do exhausting physical work

Industrial Revolution the growth in factory work in the 1800s, when new power-driven machinery was first used in place of man-power

malice wanting to do harm

mental asylum a special secure hospital for people with disturbed minds and behaviour

Don't be a dunce, learn the words!

mercury (poisoning) a poisonous metal once used in making felt for hats

poaching hunting or killing protected wildlife; a way of cooking eggs in water

public schools schools that charge fees – often boarding schools for children from rich families

rapscallion a rascal – a mean or dishonest person

respectable behaving in a decent and correct way

scallywag a rascal – a mean or dishonest person

skulduggery sneaky or dishonest behaviour

slaughter houses where farm animals are killed for meat

sterilise to clean away all dirt and germs

straitjacket a strong canvas cover tied round a person's body to stop them moving their arms, used to control violent prisoners

typhoid a disease and fever passed from one person to another

urchins poor children who are dirty and dressed in rags

workhouse where poor people went when they had no money or anywhere to live. The rules were strict and men, women and children were kept apart

Weird Websites

Pssst. There's something you need to know.
This book is a fun look at just some of the mad, bad and dangerous Victorian goings-on. For more Victorian facts, fun and games take a peep at:

www.bbc.co.uk/schools/
primaryhistory/victorian_britain/
Try the Time Capsule game!

www.victorianschool.co.uk/
great%20victorians.html
Meet some amazing Victorians!

www.youtube.com/
watch?v=2u5Bu9BsMgM
Sing along with Queen Victoria
and Prince Albert!

www.nationalarchives.gov.uk/
education/victorianbritain/
default.htm
What it was really like in
Victorian times...

Infernal Index

A

Albert (Prince) 11
  death 54
arsenic 64

B

Barnardo, Thomas 30
Bobbies (police) 62
Brown, John (friend and
  servant) 8, 84

C

cholera 53, 56, 68, 86
corsets 20–21
crime, punishments 63, 67,
  68–69

D

dead bodies 13
death masks 12
Dickens, Charles 40
diseases 55, 56, 57
dredgermen 13
dysentry 53

F

Factory Acts 28
fashion 11, 20–21

G

Great Stink 57

I

inventions 72
  all-weather unicycle 77
  Christmas cards 74
  hands-free reader 79
  moustache protector 78
  Penny Black (stamp) 74
  safety coffin 86, 87
  sea boots 76
  stamp licker 74
  telephone 72
  water closet 75

J

Jack the Ripper 65

L

left-handed 32

M

manners, children 16
  gentlemen 17
  women 18–19

N

Nightingale, Florence 52–53

P

Peel, Robert 62
phossy jaw 31
police 13, 62
poor 12, 28–29, 30–31, 66–67
prisons 67, 68

R

Ragged School 30

S

school, laws 32
  poor 32
  punishments 33
sea disasters 42–43, 44, 68–69
seaside holidays 18
surgery 50–51

T

toilets 48
trains, disasters 40–41,
  steam 38
  Tay Railway Bridge 41
typhoid 53, 55, 68

V

Victoria (Queen) 6, 7–8, 84–85
  assassination attempts 9, 22–23
  children 9, 34–35
  death 85
  marriage 11

W

work, children 28
  chimney sweep 29
  coal mines 28
  crossing sweeper 30
  match sellers 31
  mudlarks 66

What are we doing?

Find out on page 66.

978 1 4451 2191 8 pb   978 1 4451 2195 6 eBook

978 1 4451 2192 5 pb   978 1 4451 2196 3 eBook

978 1 4451 2193 2 pb   978 1 4451 2239 7 eBook

978 1 4451 2194 9 pb   978 1 4451 2240 3 eBook